Heaven:
A World of Love

Heaven:
A World
of Love

Calvary Press
Amityville, New York

Calvary Press
P.O. Box 805
Amityville, NY 11701
U.S.A.
1-800-789-8175
website: calvarypress.com
email: calvrypres@aol.com

ISBN 1-879737-36-1

Excerpted from *Charity and Its Fruits*, currently in print through
The Banner of Truth Trust, Carlisle, PA, USA

Cover & Page Design: Anthony Rotolo

ABOUT THE TYPE: This book was set in Galliard, a typeface designed by Matthew Carter for the Merganthaler Linotype Company in 1978. Galliard is based on the sixteenth-century typefaces of Robert Granjon, which give it classic lines yet interject a contemporary look.

Edwards, Jonathan
  Heaven—A World of Love
Recommended Dewey Decimal Classification: 234
Suggested Subject Headings:
1. Religion—Inspirational—Heaven
2. Christian literature—Inspirational—Heaven
3. Heaven—teaching literature—Jonathan Edwards
I. Title

Manufactured in the United States of America
1 2 3 4 5 6 7 8 9 10   99 00 01

Table of Contents

"If then you were raised with Christ,
seek those things which are above,
where Christ is, sitting at
the right hand of God.
Set your mind on things above,
not on things on the earth.
For you died, and your life
is hidden with Christ in God."
Colossians 3:1-3

"There is nothing but heaven
worth setting our hearts upon."
Richard Baxter

"Our duty as Christians is always
to keep heaven in our eye
and earth under our feet."
Matthew Henry

Preface

Most Christians hopefully know that Jonathan Edwards was the preacher of America's most famous sermon—*Sinners in the Hands of an Angry God,* preached at Enfield, Conn. on July 8th, 1741. Many in attendance that day were profoundly and even physically moved. No doubt, some were converted on that occasion of a mighty manifestation of our living and convicting Lord. Fewer people know that this "fundamentalist" was probably the finest theologian/philosopher America has ever known. Though Edwards was a congregationalist, a Lutheran writer rightly calls him "America's Theologian," as he is truly a gift to us all. Even fewer people know that this great preacher of hell reached the very height of his preaching in describing with powerful, biblical detail the incomparable majesty of heaven embodied in this very work.

Reader, whoever you are, I challenge you to read this and still wonder if there is a heaven! Even if you did not know that this magnificent painting was drawn from the Word of God, you would sense that it had to be. No man, however great his genius, could draw this up from the depths of human understanding. This picture of heaven had to come down from heaven. No creature could imagine such beauty. Its reality had to illumine him! Only God could conceive God, and only God could reveal His dwelling place with those whose love for Him was born of His love for them.

Edwards is known as a "scare-preacher." And he was a scare-preacher. And every faithful preacher of Jesus Christ, the greatest scare-preacher of them all, is a scare-preacher. In fact, if a preacher is not a scare-preacher, he is not a preacher of the grace of God (for in what context can the grace of God be fully understood and appreciated except by imparting to God's people the truth of the existence and horrors of eternal damnation from which God saves us).

Impenitent sinner, you *ought* to be scared, but not scared *silly*. Not out of your wits, but into them. And not just by seeing the hell you are going into, but the heaven you would be missing! Hell is the divine stick and heaven is the divine carrot—a real eternal stick or a real everlasting carrot.

It is natural, rational, *human* to hate pain and love pleasure. *"What"* Christ, not Edwards, asks, *"does it profit a man to gain the whole world and lose his own soul?"* What folly to live in loveless sin here and then experience its "wages" hereafter.

Christ offers life, even life everlasting now, when you turn from death here and hereafter! In Him you come to the heaven here described, right now!

So remember, dear unbelieving reader, dear friend, unless you repent you will perish in the hell you are already beginning to experience now in this world! And if you would enter heaven now, the Lord, whose love is the very essence of heaven, declares, **"You must be born again!"** Read on, dear reader, read on!

—Dr. John H. Gerstner, February 26, 1992

Introduction

"Love never fails. But whether there are prophecies, they will fail; whether there are tongues, they will cease; whether there is knowledge, it will vanish away. For we know in part and we prophesy in part. But when that which is perfect has come, then that which is in part will be done away."
—*1st Corinthians 13:8-10*

From the first of these verses (v. 8), I have already drawn the doctrine, that the great fruit of the Spirit in which the Holy Spirit shall not only for a season, but everlastingly, be imparted to the church of Christ, is charity or divine love.[1] And now I shall consider the same verse in connection with the two that follow it, and upon the three verses would make two observations.

First, that it is mentioned as one great excellence of love, that it shall remain when all other fruits of the Spirit have failed. And, *second,* that this will come to pass in the perfect state of the church, when that which is in part shall be done away, and that which is perfect has come.

The *doctrine* which I would desire to draw from this text is, that—*HEAVEN IS A WORLD OF DIVINE LOVE.*

The apostle speaks, in the text, of a state of the church when it is perfect in heaven, and therefore a state in which the Holy Spirit shall be more perfectly and abundantly given to the church than it is now on earth. But the way in which it shall be given when it is so abundantly poured forth, will be in that great fruit of the Spirit, holy and divine love, in the hearts of all the

9

blessed inhabitants of that world. So that the heavenly state of the church is a state that is distinguished from its earthly state, as it is that state which God has designed especially for such an impartation of His Holy Spirit, and in which it shall be given perfectly, whereas, in the present state of the church, it is given with great imperfection.[2] And it is also a state in which this holy love shall be, as it were, the only gift or fruit of the Spirit, as being the most perfect and glorious of all, and which, being brought to perfection, renders all other gifts that God was inclined to bestow on His church on earth, needless.

And that we may more readily see how heaven is thus a world of holy love, I would consider, *first*, the great cause and fountain of love that is in heaven; *second*, the objects of love that it contains; *third*, the subjects of that love; *fourth*, its principle, or the love itself; *fifth*, the excellent circumstances in which it is there exercised and expressed and enjoyed; and *sixth*, the happy effects and fruits of all this. Having considered these six headings we will conclude with several lines of application, which, under God, may be used to bring home these lessons to the heart of each hearer.

The Great Cause and Fountain of Love in Heaven

CHAPTER ONE

Here I remark that the God of love Himself dwells in heaven. Heaven is the palace or presence-chamber of the high and holy One, whose name is love, and who is both the cause and source of all holy love. God, considered with respect to His essence, is everywhere—He fills both heaven and earth. But yet He is said, in some respects, to be more especially in some places than in others. He was said of old to dwell in the land of Israel, above all other lands; and in Jerusalem, above all other cities of that land; and in the temple, above all other buildings in the city; and in the holy of holies, above all other apartments of the temple; and on the mercy-seat, over the ark of the covenant, above all other places in the holy of holies. But heaven is His dwelling-place above all other places in the universe; and all those places in which He was said to dwell of old, were but types of this. Heaven is a part of creation that God has built for this end, to be the place of His glorious presence, and it is His abode forever; and here will He dwell, and gloriously manifest Himself to all eternity.[3]

And this renders heaven a world of love; for God is the fountain of love, as the sun is the fountain of light. And therefore the glorious presence of God in heaven, fills heaven with love, as the sun, placed in the midst of the visible heavens in a clear day, fills the world with light. The apostle tells us that "God is love;" and therefore, seeing He is an infinite being, it follows that He is an infinite fountain of love. Seeing He is an all-sufficient being, it follows that He is a full and over-flowing, and inexhaustible fountain of love. And in that He is an unchangeable and eternal being, He is an unchangeable and eternal fountain of love.

There, even in heaven, dwells the God from whom every stream of holy love, yea, every drop that is, or ever was, proceeds. There dwells God the Father, God the Son, and God the Spirit, united as one in infinitely dear and incomprehensible and mutual and eternal love. There dwells God the Father, who is the Father of mercies, and so the Father of love, who so loved the world as to give His only-begotten Son to die for it. There dwells Christ, the Lamb of God, the Prince of peace and of love, who so loved the world that He shed His blood, and poured out His soul unto death for men. There dwells the great Mediator, through whom all the divine love is expressed toward men, and by whom the fruits of that love have been purchased, and through whom they are communicated, and through whom love is imparted to the hearts of all God's people. There dwells Christ in both His natures, the human and the divine, sitting on the same throne with the Father. And there dwells the Holy Spirit—the Spirit of divine love, in whom the very essence of God, as it were, flows out, and is breathed forth in love, and by whose immediate influence all holy love is shed abroad in the hearts of all the saints on earth and in heaven. There, in heaven, this infinite fountain of love—this eternal Three in One—is set open without any obstacle to hinder access to it, as it flows forever. There this glorious God is manifested, and shines forth, in full glory, in beams of love.

And there this glorious fountain forever flows forth in streams, yea, in rivers of love and delight, and these rivers swell, as it were, to an ocean of love, in which the souls of the ransomed may bathe with the sweetest enjoyment, and their hearts, as it were, be deluged with love, and that forever!

The Objects of Love That Heaven Contains

CHAPTER TWO

And here I would observe three things—

1. *There are none but lovely objects in heaven.* No offensive or unlovely or polluted person or thing is to be seen there. There is nothing there that is wicked or unholy. "There shall in no wise enter into it anything that defileth, neither whatsoever worketh abomination" (Rev. 21:27). And there is nothing that is deformed with any natural or moral deformity;[4] but everything is beautiful to behold and amiable and excellent in itself. The God that dwells and gloriously manifests Himself there, is infinitely lovely; gloriously lovely as a heavenly Father, as a divine Redeemer, and as a holy Sanctifier.

All the persons that belong to the blessed society of heaven are lovely. The Father of the family is lovely and so are all His children; the Head of the body lovely, and so are all the members. Among the angels there are none that are unlovely—for they are all holy; and no evil angels are permitted to infest heaven as they do this world, but they are kept forever at a distance by that great gulf which is between them and the glorious world of love. And among all the company of the saints, there are no unlovely persons. There are no false professors or hypocrites there; none that pretend to be saints, and yet are of an unchristian and hateful spirit or behavior, as is often the case in this world; none whose gold has not been purified from its dross; none who are not lovely in themselves and to others. There is no one object there to give offence, or at any time to give occasion for any passion or emotion of hatred or dislike, but every object there shall draw forth love forever and ever.

2. *They shall be not just lovely, but perfectly lovely.* [5] There are many things in this world that in the general are lovely, but yet are not perfectly free from that which is the contrary. There are spots on the sun; and so there are many men that are most amiable and worthy to be loved, who yet are not without some things that are offensive and unlovely. Often there is in good men some defect of disposition or character or conduct that mars the excellence of what otherwise would seem most amiable; and even the very best of men, are, on earth, imperfect. But it is not so in heaven. There shall be no pollution or deformity or offensive defect of any kind, seen in any person or thing; but every one shall be perfectly pure, and perfectly lovely in heaven. That blessed world shall be perfectly bright, without any darkness; perfectly fair, without any spot; perfectly clear, without any cloud. No moral or natural defect shall ever enter there; and there nothing will be seen that is sinful or weak or foolish; nothing, the nature or aspect of which is coarse or displeasing, or that can offend the most refined taste or the most delicate eye. In that blessed place no string shall vibrate out of tune, to cause any jar in the harmony of the music of heaven; and no note be such as to make discord in the anthems of saints and angels.

The great God who so fully manifests Himself there is perfect with an absolute and infinite perfection. The Son of God, who is the brightness of the Father's glory, appears there in the fullness of His glory without that garb of outward lowliness in which He appeared in this world. The Holy Spirit shall there be poured forth with perfect richness and sweetness, as a pure river of the water of life, clear as crystal, proceeding out of the throne of God and of the Lamb. And every member of that holy and blessed society shall be without any stain of sin or imperfection or weakness or impropriety or blemish of any kind. The whole church, ransomed and purified, shall there be presented to Christ, as a bride, clothed in fine linen, clean and white, without spot, or wrinkle, or any such thing. Wherever the inhabitants of that blessed world shall turn their eyes, they shall see nothing but dignity, and beauty, and glory. The most impressive and stately cities on earth, however magnificent their buildings, yet have their foundations in the dust, and their streets dirty and defiled, and made to be trodden under foot; but the very streets of this heavenly city are of pure gold, like unto transparent glass, and its foundations are of precious stones, and its gates are pearls (Revelation 21). And all these are but faint emblems of the purity and perfectness of those that dwell therein.

3. *And in heaven, shall be all those objects that the saints have set their hearts upon, and which they have loved above all things while in this world.* There they will find those things that appeared most lovely to them while they dwelt on earth; the things that met the approval of their judgments, and captivated their affections, and drew away their souls from the most dear and pleasant of earthly objects. There they will find those things that were their delight here below, and on which they rejoiced to meditate, and with the sweet contemplation of which their minds were often entertained. There, too, they shall readily find the things which they chose for their portion, and which were so dear to them that they were ready for the sake of them to undergo the severest sufferings, and to forsake even father, and mother, and family, and friends, and wife, and children, and life itself. All the truly great and good, all the pure and holy and excellent from this world, and it may be from every part of the universe, are constantly tending toward heaven. As the streams tend to the ocean, so all these are tending to the great ocean of infinite purity and bliss. The progress of time does but bear them on to its blessedness; and us, if we are holy, to be united to them there. Every gem which death rudely tears away from us here is a glorious jewel forever shining there. Every Christian friend that goes before us from this world, is a ransomed spirit waiting to welcome us in heaven. There will be the infant of days that we have lost below, through grace to be found above. There the Christian father, and mother, and wife, and child, and friend, with whom we shall renew the holy fellowship of the saints, which was interrupted by death here, but shall be commenced again in the upper sanctuary, and then shall never end. There we shall have companionship with the patriarchs and fathers and saints of the Old and New Testaments, and those of whom the world was not worthy, with whom on earth we were only conversant by faith. And there, above all, we shall enjoy and dwell with God the Father, whom we have loved with all our hearts on earth; and with Jesus Christ, our beloved Savior, who has always been to us the chief among ten thousands, and altogether lovely; and with the Holy Spirit, our Sanctifier, and Guide, and Comforter; and shall be filled with all the fullness of the Godhead forever!

The Subjects

of Love

in Heaven

CHAPTER THREE

And such being the objects of love in heaven, I pass to its *subjects*; and these are, *the hearts in which it dwells.*—In every heart in heaven, love dwells and reigns. The heart of God is the original seat or subject of love. Divine love is in Him, not as in a subject that receives it from another, but as in its original seat, where it is of itself. Love is in God, as light is in the sun, which does not shine by a reflected light, as the moon and planets do, but by its own light, and as the great fountain of light. And from God, love flows out toward all the inhabitants of heaven. It flows out, in the first place, necessarily and infinitely, toward his only-begotten Son; being poured forth, without mixture, as to an object that is infinite, and so fully adequate to all the fullness of a love that is infinite. And this infinite love is infinitely exercised toward Him. Not only does the fountain send forth streams to this object, but the very fountain itself wholly and altogether goes out toward Him. And the Son of God is not only the infinite object of love, but He is also an infinite subject of it. He is not only the Beloved of the Father, but He infinitely loves Him. The infinite essential love of God, is, as it were, an infinite and eternal, mutual, holy, energy between the Father and the Son: a pure and holy act, whereby the Deity becomes, as it were, one infinite and unchangeable emotion of love proceeding from both the Father and the Son. This divine love has its seat in the Deity, as it is exercised within the Deity, or in God toward Himself.

But this love is not confined to such exercises as these. It flows out in innumerable streams toward all the created inhabitants of heaven, to all the saints and angels there. The love of God the Father flows out toward Christ the head, and to all the members through Him, in whom they were beloved before the foundation of the world, and in whom the Father's love was expressed toward them in time, by His death and sufferings, as it now is fully manifested in heaven. And the saints and angels are secondarily the subjects of holy love, not as those in whom it is as in an original seat, as light is in the sun, but as it is in the planets, that shine only by reflected light. And the light of their love is reflected in the first place, and chiefly, back to its great source. As God has given the saints and angels love, so their love is chiefly exercised towards God its fountain, as is most reasonable. They all love God with a supreme love. There is no enemy of God in heaven; but all, as His children, love Him as their Father. They are all united, with one mind, to breathe forth their whole souls in love to God their eternal Father, and to Jesus Christ their common Redeemer, and Head, and Friend.[6]

Christ loves all His saints in heaven. His love flows out to His whole church there, and to every individual member of it. And they all, with one heart and one soul, unite in love to their common Redeemer. Every heart is wedded to this holy and spiritual Husband, and all rejoice in Him, while the angels join them in their love. And the angels and saints all love each other. All the members of the glorious society of heaven are sincerely united.

There is not a single secret or open enemy among them all. Not one heart is there that is not full of love, and not a solitary inhabitant that is not beloved by all the others. And as all are lovely, so all see each other's loveliness with full contentment and delight. Every soul goes out in love to every other; and among all the blessed inhabitants, love is mutual, and full, and eternal.

The Principle

or Essence

of Love

in Heaven

CHAPTER FOUR

And by this I mean, *the love itself* that fills and blesses the heavenly world, and which may be noticed both as to its nature and degree.

1. *As to its nature*[7]—This love is altogether holy and divine. Most of the love that there is in this world is of an unhallowed nature. But the love that has place in heaven is not carnal but spiritual. It does not proceed from corrupt principles or selfish motives, nor is it directed to low and vile purposes and ends. As opposed to all this, it is a pure flame, directed by holy motives, and aiming at no ends inconsistent with God's glory and the happiness of the universe. The saints in heaven love God for His own sake, and each other for God's sake, and for the sake of the relation that they have to Him, and the image of God that is upon them. All their love is pure and holy. We may notice this love, also,

2. *As to its degree*—And in degree it is perfect. The love that dwells in the heart of God is perfect, with an absolutely infinite and divine perfection. The love of angels and saints to God and Christ, is perfect in its kind, or with such a perfection as is proper to their nature. It is perfect with a sinless perfection, and perfect in that it is consistent with the capacities of their nature. So it is said in the text, that "when that which is perfect is come, that which is in part shall be done away" (v. 10). Their love shall be without any remains of any contrary principle, having no pride or selfishness to interrupt it or hinder its exercises. Their hearts shall be full of love. That which was in the heart on earth as but a grain of mustard-seed, shall be as a great tree in heaven. The soul that in this world had only a little spark of divine love in it, in heaven shall be, as it were, turned into a bright and ardent flame, like the sun in its fullest brightness, when it has no spot upon it.

In heaven there shall be no remaining enmity or distaste or coldness or deadness of heart towards God and Christ. Not the least remainder of any principle of envy shall exist to be exercised toward angels or other beings who are superior in glory; nor shall there be anything like contempt or slighting of those who are inferiors. Those that have a lower station in glory than others, suffer no lessening of their own happiness by seeing others above them in glory. On the contrary, all the members of that blessed society rejoice in each other's happiness, for the love of benevolence is perfect in them all. Every one has not only a sincere, but a perfect good-will to every other. Sincere and strong love is greatly gratified and delighted in the prosperity of the beloved object; and if the love be perfect, the greater the prosperity of the beloved is, the more is the lover pleased and delighted; for the prosperity of the beloved is, as it were, the food of love, and therefore the greater that prosperity, the more richly is love feasted. The love of benevolence is delighted in beholding the prosperity of another, in the same way that the love of contentment is, in beholding the beauty or perfection of another. So that the superior prosperity of those that are higher in glory, is so far from being a hindrance to the degree of love felt toward them, that it is an addition to it, or a part of it.

There is undoubtedly an inconceivably pure, sweet, and fervent love between the saints in glory; and that love is in proportion to the perfection and amiableness of the objects beloved. Therefore it must necessarily cause delight in them when they see that the happiness and glory of others are in proportion to their amiableness, and so in proportion to their love to them. Those that are highest in glory, are those that are highest in holiness, and therefore are those that are most beloved by all the saints; for they most love those that are most holy, and so they will all rejoice in their being the most happy. And it will not be a grief to any of the saints to see those that are higher than themselves in holiness and likeness to God, more loved also than themselves. For all shall have as much love as they desire, and as great manifestations of love as they can bear. And in this manner, all shall be fully satisfied. And where there is perfect satisfaction, there can be no reason for envy. And there will be no temptation for any to envy those that are above them in glory, on account of the latter being lifted up with pride; for there will be no pride in heaven. We are not to conceive that those who are more holy and happy than others in heaven, will be elated and lifted up in their spirit above others; for those who are above others in holiness, will be superior to them in humility. The saints that are highest in glory will be the lowest in humbleness of mind, for their superior humility is part of their superior holiness. Though all are perfectly free from pride, yet, as some will have greater degrees of divine knowledge than others, and larger capacities to see more of the divine perfections, so they will see more of their own comparative little-ness and nothingness, and therefore will be lowest and most abased in humility.

And, besides, the inferior in glory will have no temp-tation to envy those that are higher than themselves, for those that are highest will not only be more loved by the lower for their higher holiness, but they will also have more of the spirit of love to others, and so will love those that are below them more than if their own capacity and elevation were less. They that are highest in degree in glory, will be of the highest capacity; and so having the greatest knowledge, will see most of God's loveliness, and consequently will have love to God and love to the saints most abounding in their hearts. And on this account those that are lower in glory will not envy those that are above them, because they will be most beloved by those that are highest in glory. And the superior in glory will be so far from slighting those that are inferior, that they will have most abundant love to them—greater degrees of love in proportion to their superior knowledge and happiness. The higher any are in glory, the more they are like Christ in this respect, so that the love of the higher to the lower will be greater than the love of the equals of the latter to them. And what puts it beyond all doubt that seeing the superior happiness of others will not be a hindrance to the happiness of the inferior, is this, that their su-perior happiness consists in their greater humility, and in their greater love to them, and to God, and to Christ, than the inferior will have in themselves. Such will be the sweet and perfect harmony among the heav-enly saints, and such the perfect love reigning in every heart toward every other, without limit or restriction, or interruption. And no envy, or malice, or revenge, or contempt, or selfishness shall ever enter there, but all such feelings shall be kept as far away as sin is from holiness, and as hell is from heaven![8]

The Excellent Circumstances Attending Love in Heaven

CHAPTER FIVE

Let us next consider, *the excellent circumstances in which love shall be exercised, expressed and enjoyed in heaven.*

1. *Love in heaven is always mutual.* It is always met with appropriate returns of love—with returns that are proportioned to its exercise. Such returns, love always seeks; and just in proportion as any person is beloved, in the same proportion is his love desired and prized. And in heaven this desire of love, or this fondness for being loved, will never fail of being satisfied. No inhabitants of that blessed world will ever be grieved with the thought that they are slighted by those that they love, or that their love is not fully and fondly returned.

As the saints will love God with an inconceivable ardency of heart, and to the utmost of their capacity, so they will know that He has loved them from all eternity, and still loves them, and will continue to love them forever. And God will then gloriously manifest Himself to them, and they shall know that all that happiness and glory which they are possessed of, are the fruits of His love. And with the same ardor and fervency will the saints love the Lord Jesus Christ; and their love will be accepted; and they shall know that He has loved them with a faithful, yea, even with a dying love. They shall then be more aware than they are now, of the great love that was manifested in Christ that He should lay down His life for them. And then will Christ open to their view the great fountain of love in His heart for them, beyond all that they ever saw before. Hereby the love of the saints to God and Christ is understood to be reciprocated, and that declaration fulfilled, "I love them that love me;" and though the love of God to them cannot properly be called the return of love, because He loved them first, yet the sight of His love, for that very reason, will fill them with greater joy, admiration and love to Him.

The love of the saints, one to another, will always be mutual and reciprocated, though we cannot suppose that every one will, in all respects, be equally beloved. Some of the saints are more beloved of God than others, even on earth. The angel told Daniel that he was "a man greatly beloved" (Dan. 9:23); and Luke is called "the beloved physician" (Col. 4:14); and John, "the disciple whom Jesus loved" (John 20:2). And so, doubtless, those that have been most eminent in fidelity and holiness, and that are highest in glory, are most beloved by Christ in heaven; and doubtless those saints that are most beloved of Christ, and that are nearest to Him in glory, are most beloved by all the other saints. Thus we may conclude that saints such as the apostle Paul and the apostle John are more beloved by the saints in heaven than other saints of lower rank. They are more beloved by lower saints than those of equal rank with themselves. But then there are appropriate returns of love in these cases; for as such are more beloved by all other saints, so they are fuller of love to other saints. The heart of Christ, the great Head of all the saints, is more full of love than the heart of any saint can be. He loves all the saints far more than any of them love each other. But the more any saint is loved of Him, the more is that saint like Him, in this respect, that his heart is more filled with love.

2. *The joy of heavenly love shall never be interrupted or stifled by jealousy.* Heavenly lovers will have no doubt of the love of each other. They shall have no fear that the declarations and professions of love are hypocritical; but shall be perfectly satisfied of the sincerity and strength of each other's affection, as much as if there were a window in every breast, so that everything in the heart could be seen. There shall be no such thing as flattery or insincerity in heaven, but there perfect sincerity shall reign through all and in all. Every one will be just what he seems to be, and will really have all the love that he seems to have. It will not be as in this world, where comparatively few things are what they seem to be, and where professions are often made lightly and without meaning. But there, every expression of love shall come from the bottom of the heart, and all that is professed shall be really and truly felt.

The saints shall know that God loves them, and they shall never doubt the greatness of His love, and they shall have no doubt of the love of all their fellow-inhabitants in heaven. And they shall not be jealous of the steadfastness of each other's love. They shall have no suspicion that the love which others have felt toward them is abated, or in any degree withdrawn from themselves for the sake of some rival, or because of anything in themselves which they suspect is distasteful to others, or through any fickleness in their own hearts or the hearts of others. Nor will they be in the least afraid that the love of any will ever be abated toward them. There shall be no such thing as fickleness and unfaithfulness in heaven, to molest and disturb the friendship of that blessed society. The saints shall have no fear that the love of God will ever abate towards them, or that Christ will not continue always to love them with unabated tenderness and affection. And they shall have no jealousy one of another, but shall know that by divine grace the mutual love that exists between them shall never decay nor change.

3. *There shall be nothing within themselves to block or hinder the saints in heaven in the exercises and expressions of love.* In this world the saints find much to hinder them in this respect. They have a great deal of dulness and heaviness. They carry about with them a heavy-molded body—a clump of earth—a mass of flesh and blood that is not fitted to be the organ for a soul inflamed with high exercises of divine love; but which is found a great impediment and hindrance to the spirit, so that they cannot express their love to God as they would, and cannot be so active and lively in it as they desire. Often they would joyfully fly, but they are held down as with a dead weight upon their wings. Gladly would they be active, and mount up, as a flame of fire, but they find themselves, as it were, hampered and chained down, so that they cannot do as their love inclines them to do. Love disposes them to burst forth in praise, but their tongues are not obedient. They lack words to express the intense passion of their souls, and cannot order their speech by reason of darkness (Job 37:19). And often, for lack of appropriate expressions, they are forced to content themselves with groanings that cannot be uttered (Romans 8:26).

But in heaven they shall have no such hindrance.

There they will have no dulness and awkwardness, and no corruption of heart to war against divine love, and hinder its expressions; and there no earthly body shall encumber the heavenly flame with its heaviness. The saints in heaven shall have no difficulty in expressing all their love. Their souls being on fire with holy love, shall not be like a fire pent up, but like a flame uncovered and at liberty. Their spirits, being winged with love, shall have no weight upon them to hinder their flight. There shall be no lack of strength or activity, nor any lack of words with which to praise the Object of their affection. Nothing shall hinder them from communing with God, and praising and serving Him just as their love inclines them to do. Love naturally desires to express itself; and in heaven the love of the saints shall be at full liberty to express itself as it desires, whether it be towards God or to created beings.

4. *In heaven love will be expressed with perfect decency and wisdom.* Many in this world that are sincere in their hearts, and have indeed a principle of true love to God and their neighbor, yet have not discretion to guide them in the manner and circumstances of expressing it. Their intentions, and so their speeches, are good, but often not suitably timed, nor discreetly ordered regarding the circumstances, but are attended with an imprudence that greatly obscures the loveliness of grace in the eyes of others. But in heaven the amiableness and excellence of their love shall not be obscured by any such means. There shall be no indecent or unwise or dissonant speeches or actions—no foolish and sentimental fondness—no needless meddlesomeness—no low or sinful inclinations of passion—and no such thing as affections clouding or deluding reason, or going before or against it. But wisdom and discretion shall be as perfect in the saints as love is, and every expression of their love shall be attended with the most amiable and perfect decency and discretion and wisdom.

5. *There shall be nothing external in heaven to keep its inhabitants at a distance from each other, or to hinder their most perfect enjoyment of each other's love.* There shall be no wall of separation in heaven to keep the saints divided, nor shall they be hindered from the full and complete enjoyment of each other's love by distance of habitation; for they shall all be together, as one family, in their heavenly Father's house. Nor shall there be any lack of full acquaintance to hinder the greatest possible intimacy; and much less shall there be any misunderstanding between them, or misinterpreting things that are said or done by each other. There shall be no disharmony through difference of disposition, or manners, or circumstances, or from various opinions, interests, feelings or alliances. But all shall be united in the same interest, and all alike allied to the same Savior, and all employed in the same business, serving and glorifying the same God.

6. *In heaven all shall be united together in very near and dear relations.* Love always seeks a near relation to the one who is beloved; and in heaven they shall all be closely allied and related to each other. All shall be closely related to God the supreme object of their love, for they shall all be His children. And all shall be closely related to Christ, for He shall be the Head of the whole society, and the Husband of the whole Church of saints, all of whom together shall constitute His spouse. And they shall all be related to each other as brethren, for all will be but one society, or rather but one family, and all members of the household of God. And more than this,

7. *In heaven all shall have property and ownership in each other.* Love seeks to have the beloved its own; and divine love rejoices in saying, "My beloved is mine, and I am his." And in heaven all shall not only be related one to another, but they shall be each other's, and belong to each other. The saints shall be God's. He brings them home to Himself in glory, as that part of the creation that He has chosen for His peculiar treasure. And on the other hand, God shall be theirs, made over to them in an everlasting covenant in this world, and now they shall be forever in full possession of Him as their portion. And so the saints shall be Christ's, for He has bought them with a price. And He shall be theirs, for He that gave Himself for them will have given Himself to them; and in the bonds of mutual and everlasting love, Christ and the saints will have given themselves to each other. And just as God and Christ shall be the saints', so the angels shall be their angels, as is intimated in Matt. 18:10; and the saints shall be one another's, for the apostle speaks (2 Cor. 8:5) of the saints in his days, as first giving themselves to the Lord, and then to one another by the will of God. And if this is done on earth, it will be more perfectly done in heaven.

8. *In heaven they shall enjoy each other's love in perfect and uninterrupted prosperity.* What often on earth diminishes the pleasure and sweetness of worldly pleasure, is, that though persons live in love, yet they live in poverty, or meet with great difficulties and bitter afflictions, whereby they are grieved for themselves and for one another. For, though in such cases love and friendship in some respects lighten the burden to be borne, yet in other respects they rather add to its weight, because those that love each other become, by their very love, sharers in each other's afflictions, so that each has not only his own trials to bear, but those also of his afflicted friends. But there shall be no adversity in heaven, to give occasion for a piteous grief of spirit, or to molest or disturb those who are heavenly friends in the enjoyment of each other's friendship. But they shall enjoy one another's love in the greatest prosperity, and in glorious riches and comfort, and in the highest honor and dignity, reigning together in the heavenly kingdom—inheriting all things, sitting on thrones, all wearing crowns of life, and being made kings and priests unto God forever.

Christ and His disciples, while on earth, were often together in affliction and trial, and they kept up and manifested the strongest love and friendship to each other under great and painful sufferings. And now in heaven they enjoy each other's love in immortal glory, all sorrow and sighing having forever fled away. Both Christ and His saints were acquainted with much sorrow and grief in this world, though Christ had the greatest share, being preeminently a "man of sorrows." But in heaven they shall sit together in heavenly places, where sorrow and grief shall never more be known. And so all the saints will enjoy each other's love in heaven, in glory and prosperity in comparison with which the wealth and thrones of the greatest earthly princes are but as wretched poverty and destitution. So that as they love one another, they have not only their own but each other's prosperity to rejoice in, and are by love made partakers of each other's blessedness and glory. Such is the love of every saint to every other saint, that it makes the glory which he sees other saints enjoy, as it were, his very own. He so rejoices that they enjoy such glory, that it is in some respects as if he himself enjoyed it in his own personal experience (see 1st Cor. 12:26).

9. *In heaven all things shall combine to promote their love, and give advantage for mutual enjoyment.* There shall be none there to tempt any to dislike or hatred; no busybodies, or malicious adversaries, to make intentional misrepresentations, or create misunderstandings, or spread abroad any evil reports, but every being and every thing shall combine to promote love, and the full enjoyment of love. Heaven itself, the place of habitation, is a garden of pleasures, a heavenly paradise, fitted in all respects for an abode of heavenly love; a place where they may have sweet society and perfect enjoyment of each other's love. None are unsocial or distant from each other. The petty distinctions of this world do not draw lines in the society of heaven, but all meet in the equality of holiness and of holy love.

All things in heaven do also remarkably show forth the beauty and loveliness of God and Christ, and have the brightness and sweetness of divine love upon them. The very light that shines in and fills that world, is the light of love, for it is the shining of the glory of the Lamb of God, that most wonderful influence of lamb-like meekness and love that fills the heavenly Jerusalem with light. "The city had no need of the sun, neither of the moon, to shine in it; for the glory of God did lighten it, and the Lamb is the light thereof" (Rev. 21:23). The glory that is about Him that reigns in heaven is so radiant and sweet, that it is compared (Rev. 4:3) to "a rainbow round about the throne, in sight like unto an emerald;" and it is the rainbow that is so often used in the Old Testament as the fit token of God's love and grace manifested in His covenant. The light of the New Jerusalem, which is the light of God's glory, is said to be like a jasper stone, clear as crystal (Rev. 21:11), thus signifying the greatest preciousness and beauty; and as to its continuance, it is said there is no night there, but only an endless and glorious day. Thus suggests, once more, that,—

10. *The inhabitants of heaven shall all know that they will continue in the perfect enjoyment of each other's love forever.* They shall know that God and Christ shall be forever with them as their God and portion, and that His love shall be continued and fully manifested forever, and that all their beloved fellow-saints shall forever live with them in glory, and shall forever keep up the same love in their hearts which they now have. And they shall know that they themselves shall ever live to love God, and love the saints, and to enjoy their love in all its fullness and sweetness forever. They shall be in

no fear of any end to this happiness, or of any abatement from its fullness and blessedness, or that they shall ever be weary of its exercises and expressions, or overindulged with its enjoyments, or that the beloved objects shall ever grow old or disagreeable, so that their love shall at last die away. All in heaven shall flourish in immortal youth and freshness. In that glorious place, age will not diminish anyone's beauty or vigor; and love shall abide in every one's heart, as a living spring perpetually springing up in the soul, or as a flame that never dies away. And the holy pleasure of this love shall be as a river that is forever flowing clear and full, and increasing continually. The heavenly paradise of love shall always be kept as in a perpetual spring, without autumn or winter, where no frosts shall blight, or leaves decay and fall, but where every plant shall be in perpetual freshness, and bloom, and fragrance, and beauty, always springing forth, and always blossoming, and always bearing fruit. The leaf of the righteous shall not wither (Psalm 1:3). And in the midst of the streets of heaven, and on either side of the river, grows the tree of life, which bears twelve manner of fruits, and yields her fruit every month (Rev. 22:2). Everything in the heavenly world shall contribute to the joy of the saints, and every joy of heaven shall be eternal. No night shall settle down with its darkness upon the brightness of their everlasting day.

The Happy

Effects and Fruits

of Love

in Heaven

CHAPTER SIX

Having thus noticed many of the blessed circumstances with which love in heaven is exercised, expressed and enjoyed, I proceed, as proposed, to speak, lastly, *of the blessed effects and fruits of this love, as exercised and enjoyed in these several circumstances.* And of the many blessed fruits of it, I would at this time mention but two.

1. *The most excellent and perfect behavior of all the inhabitants of heaven toward God and each other.* Charity, or divine love, is the sum of all good principles, and therefore the fountain from which proceed all amiable and excellent actions. And just as in heaven this love will be perfect, to the perfect exclusion of all sin consisting in enmity against God and fellow-creatures, so the fruit of it will be a most perfect behavior toward all. Hence life in heaven will be without the least sinful

failure or error. None shall ever come short, or turn aside from the way of holiness in the least degree, but every feeling and action shall be perfect in itself and in all its circumstances. Every part of their behavior shall be holy and divine in matter, and form, and spirit, and end.

We know not particularly how the saints in heaven shall be employed; but in general we know that they are employed in praising and serving God; and this they will do perfectly, being influenced by such a love as we have been considering. And we have reason to think that they are so employed as in some way to be subservient, under God, to each other's happiness, for they are represented in the Scriptures as united together in one society, which, it would seem, can be for no other purpose but mutual subserviency and happiness. And they are thus mutually subservient by a most excellent and perfectly amiable behavior one towards another, as a fruit of their perfect love one to another. And even if they are not confined to this society, but if any or all of them are at times sent on errands of duty or mercy to distant worlds, or employed, as some suppose them to be, as ministering spirits to friends in this world, they are still led by the influence of love, to conduct themselves, in all their behavior, in such a manner as is well pleasing to God, and thus conducive to their own and others' happiness. Now the other fruit of love, as exercised in such circumstances, is,

2. Perfect tranquillity and joy in heaven.[9] Charity, or holy and humble Christian love, is a principle of wonderful power to give indescribable quietness and tranquillity to the soul. It banishes all disturbance, and sweetly composes and brings rest to the spirit, and makes all divinely calm and sweet and happy. In that soul where divine love reigns and is in lively exercise, nothing can cause a storm, or even gather threatening clouds.

There are many principles contrary to love, that make this world like a tempestuous sea. Selfishness, and envy, and revenge, and jealousy, and kindred passions keep life on earth in a constant tumult, and make it a scene of confusion and uproar, where no quiet rest is to be enjoyed except in renouncing this world and looking to another. But oh! what rest there is in that world which the God of peace and love fills with His own gracious presence, and in which the Lamb of God lives and reigns, filling it with the brightest and sweetest beams of His love; where there is nothing to disturb or offend, and no being or object to be seen that is not surrounded with perfect amiableness and sweetness; where the saints shall find and enjoy all that they love, and so be perfectly satisfied; where there is no enemy and no enmity, but perfect love in every heart and to every being; where there is perfect harmony among all the inhabitants, no one envying another, but every one rejoicing in the happiness of every other; where all their love is humble and holy, and perfectly Christian, without the least carnality or impurity; where love is always mutual and reciprocated to the full; where there is no hypocrisy or deception, but perfect simplicity and sincerity; where there is no treachery, or unfaithfulness, or fickleness, or jealousy in any form; where there is no obstacle or hindrance to the exercises or expressions of love, no imprudence or indecency in expressing it, and no influence of folly or indiscretion in any word or deed; where there is no separation wall, and no misunderstanding or strangeness, but full acquaintance and perfect intimacy in all; where there is no division through different opinions or interests, but where all in that glorious and loving society shall be most nearly and divinely related, and each shall belong to every other, and all shall enjoy each other in perfect prosperity and riches, and honor, without any sickness, or grief, or persecution, or sorrow, or any enemy to molest them, or any busybody to create jealousy or misunderstanding, or mar the perfect, and holy, and blessed peace that reigns in heaven! And all this in the garden of God—in the paradise of love, where everything is filled with love, and everything combines to promote and kindle it, and keep up its flame, and nothing ever interrupts it, but everything has been fitted by an all-wise God for its full enjoyment under the greatest advantages forever! And all, too, where the beauty of the beloved objects shall never fade, and love shall never grow weary nor decay, but the soul shall more and more rejoice in love forever!

Oh! what tranquillity will there be in such a world as this! And who can express the fullness and blessedness of this peace! What a calm is this! How sweet, and holy, and joyous! What a haven of rest to enter, after having passed through the storms and tempests of this world, in which pride, and selfishness, and envy, and malice, and scorn, and contempt, and contention, and vice, are as waves of a restless ocean, always rolling, and often dashed about in violence and fury! What a Canaan of rest to come to, after going through this waste and howling wilderness, full of snares, and pitfalls, and poisonous serpents, where no rest could be found!

And oh! what joy will there be, springing up in the hearts of the saints, after they have passed through their wearisome pilgrimage, to be brought to such a paradise as this! Here is joy unspeakable indeed, and full of glory—joy that is humble, holy, enrapturing, and divine in its perfection! Love is always a sweet principle; and especially divine love. This, even on earth, is a spring of sweetness; but in heaven it shall become a stream, a river, an ocean! All shall stand about the God of glory, who is the great fountain of love, opening, as it were, their very souls to be filled with those effusions of love that are poured forth from His fullness, just as the flowers on the earth, in the bright and joyous days of spring, open their bosoms to the sun, to be filled with his light and warmth, and to flourish in beauty and fragrancy under his cheering rays.

Every saint in heaven is as a flower in that garden of God, and holy love is the fragrance and sweet odor that they all send forth, and with which they fill the arbors of that paradise above. Every soul there, is as a note in some concert of delightful music, that sweetly harmonizes with every other note, and all together blend in the most rapturous strains in praising God and the Lamb forever. And so all help each other, to their utmost, to express the love of the whole society to its glorious Father and Head, and to pour back love into the great fountain of love from which they are supplied and filled with love, and blessedness, and glory. And thus they will love, and reign in love, and in that godlike joy that is its blessed fruit, such as eye hath not seen, nor ear heard, nor hath ever entered into the heart of man in this world to conceive. And thus in the full sunlight of the throne, enraptured with joys that are forever increasing, and yet forever full, they shall live and reign with God and Christ forever and ever!

What Marks Are Found Upon Those Who Will Inhabit Heaven?

CHAPTER SEVEN

In the application of this subject, I remark,

1. *If heaven is such a world as has been described, then we may see a reason why contention and strife tend to darken our evidence of fitness for its possession.* Experience teaches that this is the effect of contention. When principles of malignity and ill-will prevail among God's people (as they sometimes do through the remaining corruption of their hearts), and they get into a contentious spirit, or are engaged in any strife whether public or private, and their spirits are filled with opposition to their neighbors in any matter whatever, their former evidences for heaven seem to become dim, or die away, and they are in darkness about their spiritual state, and do not find that comfortable and satisfying hope that they used to enjoy.

And so, when converted persons get into ill frames in their families, the consequence commonly, if not universally, is, that they live without much of a comfortable sense of heavenly things, or any lively hope of heaven. They do not enjoy much of that spiritual calm and sweetness that those do who live in love and peace. They have not that help from God, and that communion with Him, and that near intercourse with heaven in prayer, that others have. The apostle Peter seems to speak of contention in families as having this influence. His language is, "Likewise, you husbands, dwell with them" (your wives) "according to knowledge, giving honor unto the wife, as unto the weaker vessel; and as being heirs together of the grace of life, *that* your prayers be not hindered" (1st Pet. 3:7). Here he intimates that discord in families tends to hinder Christians in their prayers. And what Christian that has made the sad experiment, has not done it to his sorrow, and in his own experience does not bear witness to the truth of the apostle's intimation?

Why it is so, that contention has this effect of hindering spiritual exercises and comforts and hopes, and of destroying the sweet hope of that which is heavenly, we may learn from the doctrine we have considered. For heaven being a world of love, it follows that, when we have the least exercise of love, and the most of a contrary spirit, then we have the least of heaven, and are farthest from it in the frame of our mind. Then we have the least of the exercise of that in which consists a conformity to heaven, and a preparation for it, and what tends to it. And so, necessarily, we must have least evidence of our title to heaven, and be farthest from the comfort which such evidence affords.[10] We may see, again, from this subject,

2. *How happy those are who are entitled to heaven.* There are some persons living on earth, to whom the happiness of the heavenly world belongs as much, yea, much more than any man's earthly estate belongs to himself. They have a part and share in this world of love, and have a proper right and title to it, for they are of the number of those of whom it is written, "Blessed are those who do His commandments, that they may have the right to the tree of life, and may enter through the gates into the city" (Rev. 22:14). And, doubtless, there are such persons here among us. And oh! how happy are all such, entitled as they are to an allotment in such a world as heaven! Surely they are the blessed of the earth, and the fullness of their blessedness no language can describe, no words express. But here some may be ready to say, "Without doubt they are happy persons that have a title to such a blessed world, and are soon to enter on the eternal possession of its joys. *But who* are these persons? *How* shall they be known, and by *what* marks may they be distinguished?"

In answer to such an inquiry, I would mention Three things that belong to their character:

First, they are those that have had the principle or seed of the same love that reigns in heaven implanted in their hearts, in this world, in the work of regeneration. They are not those who have no other principles in their hearts than natural principles, or such as they have by their first birth, for "that which is born of the flesh is flesh." But they are those who have been the subjects of the new birth, or who have been born of the Spirit. A glorious work of the Spirit of God has been wrought in their hearts, renewing them by bringing down from heaven, as it were, some of the light and some of the holy, pure flame that is in that world of love, and giving it place in them. Their hearts are a soil in which this heavenly seed has been sown, and in which it abides and grows. And so they are changed, and, from being earthly, have become heavenly in their dispositions. The love of the world is mortified, and the love of God implanted. Their hearts are drawn to God and

Christ, and for their sakes flow out to the saints in humble and spiritual love. "Being born again, not of corruptible seed, but of incorruptible" (1 Pet. 1:23); "Which were born, not of blood, nor of the will of the flesh, nor of the will of man, but of God" (John 1:13).

Second, they are those who have freely chosen the happiness that flows from the exercise and enjoyment of such love as is in heaven, above all other conceivable happiness. They see and understand so much of this as to know that it is the best good. They do not merely yield that it is so from rational arguments that may be offered for it, and by which they are convinced that it is so, but they *know* it is so from what little they have tasted of it. It is the happiness of love, and the beginning of a life of such love: holy, humble, divine and heavenly love. Love to God, and love to Christ, and love to saints for God and Christ's sake, and the enjoyment of the fruits of God's love in holy communion with God, and Christ, and with holy persons—this is what they have a relish for. And such is their renewed nature, that such happiness suits their disposition and appetite and wishes above all other things. And not only above all things that they have, but above all that they can conceive it possible that they could have. The world does not afford anything like it. They have chosen this before all things else, and chosen it freely. Their souls go out after it more than after everything else, and their hearts are more eager in pursuit of it. They have chosen it not merely because they have met with sorrow, and are in such low and afflicted circumstances that they do not expect much from the world, but because their hearts were so captivated by this good that they chose it for its own sake before all worldly good, even if they could have ever so much of the latter, and enjoy it ever so long.

Third, they are those who, from the love that is in them, are, in heart and life, in principle and practice, struggling after holiness.[11] Holy love makes them long for holiness. It is a principle that thirsts after growth. This love is in imperfection, and in a state of infancy, in this world, and it desires growth. It has much to struggle with. In the heart in this world there are many opposite principles and influences; and it struggles after greater oneness, and more liberty, and more free exercise, and better fruit. The great strife and struggle of the new man is after holiness. His heart struggles after it, for he has an interest in heaven, and therefore he struggles with that sin that would keep him from it. He is full of ardent desires, and breathings, and longings, and strivings to be holy. And his hands struggle as well as his heart. He strives in his practice. His life is a life of sincere and earnest endeavor to be universally and increasingly holy. He feels that he is not holy enough, but far from it; and he desires to be nearer perfection, and more like those who are in heaven. And this is one reason why he longs to be in heaven, that he may be perfectly holy. And the great principle which leads him thus to struggle, is love. It is not only fear; but it is love to God, and love to Christ, and love to holiness. Love is a holy fire within him, and, like any other flame which is in a degree pent up, it will and does struggle for liberty; and this its struggling is the struggle for holiness.

An Alarm to Awaken the Unconverted

CHAPTER EIGHT

What has been said on this subject may well awaken and alarm the unconverted. *First, By putting them in mind of their misery, in that they have no portion or right in this world of love.* You have heard what has been said of heaven, what kind of glory and blessedness is there, and how happy the saints and angels are in that world of perfect love. But consider that none of this belongs to you, if you are unconverted. When you hear of such things, you hear of that in which you have no share. No such person as you, a wicked hater of God and Christ, and one that is under the power of a spirit of enmity against all that is good, shall ever enter there. Such as you are, never belong to the faithful Israel of God, and shall never enter their heavenly rest. It may be said to you, as Peter said to Simon, "Thou hast neither part nor lot in this matter, for thy heart is not right in the sight of God" (Acts 8:21); and as Nehemiah said to Sanballat and his associates, "You have no portion, nor right, nor memorial, in Jerusalem" (Neh. 2:20). If such a soul as yours should be admitted into heaven, that world of love, how repugnant would it be to those blessed spirits whose souls are as a flame of love! and how would it disturb that loving and blessed society, and put everything in confusion! It would make heaven no longer heaven, if such souls should be admitted there. It would change it from a world of love to a world of hatred, and pride, and envy, and malice, and revenge, as this world is! But this shall never be; and the only alternative is, that such as you shall be shut out with "dogs, and sorcerers, and whoremongers, and murderers, and idolaters, and whoever loves and makes a lie" (Rev. 22:15). That is, with all that is vile, unclean and unholy. And this subject may well awaken and alarm the unrepentant,

Secondly, By showing them that they are in danger of hell, which is a world of hatred. There are three worlds. One is this, which is an intermediate world—a world in which good and evil are so mixed together as to be a sure sign that this world is not to continue forever. Another is heaven, a world of love, without any hatred. And the other is hell, a world of hatred, where there is not love, which is the world to which all of you who are in a Christless state properly belong. This last is the world where God manifests His displeasure and wrath, as in heaven He manifests His love. Everything in hell is hateful. There is not one solitary object there that is not offensive and detestable, horrid and hateful. There is no person or thing to be seen there, that is amiable or lovely; nothing that is pure, or holy, or pleasant, but everything abominable and detestable. There are no beings there but devils, and damned spirits that are like devils. Hell is, as it were, a vast den of poisonous hissing serpents; the old serpent, who is the devil and Satan, and with him all his hateful brood.

In that dark world there are none but those whom God hates with a perfect and everlasting hatred. He exercised no love, and extends no mercy to any one object there, but pours out upon them horrors without mixture. All things in the wide universe that are hateful shall be gathered together in hell, as in a vast receptacle provided on purpose, that the universe which God has made may be cleansed of its filthiness, by casting it all into this great sink of wickedness and woe. It is a world prepared on purpose for the expression of God's wrath. He has made hell for this; and He has no other use for it but there to testify forever His hatred of sin and sinners, where there is no token of love or mercy. There is nothing there but what shows forth the Divine indignation and wrath. Every object shows forth wrath. It is a world all overflowed with a deluge of wrath, as it were, with a deluge of liquid fire, so as to be called a lake of fire and brimstone, and the second death.

There are none in hell but those who have been haters of God, and so have procured His wrath and hatred on themselves; and there they shall continue to hate Him forever. No love to God will ever be felt in hell; but everyone there perfectly hates Him, and so will continue to hate Him, and without any restraint will express their hatred to Him, blaspheming and raging against Him, while they gnaw their tongues for pain. And though they all join together in their enmity and opposition to God, yet there is no union or friendliness among themselves—they agree in nothing but hatred, and the expression of hatred. They hate God, and Christ, and angels, and saints in heaven; and not only so, but they hate one another, like a company of serpents or vipers, not only spitting out venom against God, but at one another, biting and stinging and tormenting each other.

The devils in hell will hate damned souls. They hated them while in this world, and therefore it was that with such subtlety and unflagging temptations they sought their ruin. They thirsted for the blood of their souls, because they hated them. They longed to get them in their power to torment them. They watched them as a roaring lion does his prey. Because they hated them, therefore they flew upon their souls like hell-hounds, the very instant they were parted from their bodies, full of eagerness to torment them. And now they have them in their power, they will spend eternity in torment-ing them with the utmost strength and cruelty that devils are capable of. They are, as it were, continually and eter-nally tearing these poor damned souls that are in their hands. And these latter will not only be hated and tor-mented by devils, but they will have no love or pity one towards another, but will be like devils one to another, and will, to their utmost, torment each other, being like brands in the fire, each of which helps to burn the others.

In hell all those principles will reign and rage that are contrary to love, without any restraining grace to keep them within bounds. There will be unrestrained pride, and malice, and envy, and revenge, and conten-tion in all its fury and without end, never knowing peace. The miserable inhabitants will bite and devour one an-other, as well as be enemies to God, and Christ, and holy beings. Those who, in their wickedness on earth, were compan-ions together, and had a sort of carnal friendship one for another, will there have no appear-ance of fellowship; but perfect and continual and undis-guised hatred will exist between them. As on earth they promoted each other's sins, so now in hell they will pro-mote each other's punishment. On earth they were the instruments of undoing each other's souls—there they were occupied in blowing up the fires of each other's lusts, and now they will blow forever the fires of each other's torments. They ruined one another in sinning, setting bad examples to each other, poisoning each other by wicked talk, and now they will be as much engaged in tormenting, as once they were in tempting and corrupting each other.

And there their hatred and envy, and all evil passions, will be a torment to themselves. God and Christ, whom they will hate most, and toward whom their souls will be as full of hatred as an oven is ever full of fire, will be infinitely above their reach, dwelling in infinite blessedness and glory which they cannot diminish. And they will but torment themselves by their fruitless envy of the saints and angels in heaven, whom they cannot come close to or injure in any way. And they shall have no pity from them or from anyone, for hell is looked on only with hatred, and with no pity or compassion. And thus they will be left to spend their eternity together.

Now consider, all you who are outside of Christ, and who were never born again, and who never had any blessed renovation of your hearts by the Holy Spirit implanting divine love in them, and leading you to choose the happiness that consists in holy love as your best and sweetest good, and to spend your life in struggling after holiness,—*consider your danger*, and what is before you. For this is the world to which you are condemned; and so the world to which you belong through the sentence of the law; and the world that every day and hour you are in danger of having your abode fixed in forever and ever; and the world to which, if you do not repent, you will soon go, instead of going to that blessed world of love of which you have just now heard. *Consider, Oh! Consider*, that it is indeed thus with you. These things are not cunningly-devised fables, but the great and dreadful realities of God's Word, and things that, in a little while, you will know with everlasting certainty are true. How, then, can you rest in such a predicament as you are in, and go about so carelessly from day to day, and so heedless and negligent of your precious, immortal souls? *Consider seriously these things*, and be wise for yourself, before it is too late;

before your feet stumble on the dark mountains, and
you fall into the world of wrath and hatred, where there
is weeping, and wailing, and gnashing of teeth, with
spiteful malice and rage against God, and Christ, and
one another, and with horror and anguish of spirit forever. Flee to the stronghold while you are prisoners of
hope, before the door of hope is closed, and the ago-
nies of the second death shall begin their work, and
your eternal doom is sealed![12]

An Exhortation to Earnestly Seek After Heaven

CHAPTER NINE

Let the consideration of what has been said of heaven *stir up all earnestly to seek after it.* If heaven truly is such a blessed world, then let it be our chosen country, and the inheritance that we look for and seek after. Let us turn our course this way, and press on to its possession. It is not impossible but that this glorious world may be obtained by us. It is offered to us. Though it be so excellent and blessed a country, yet God stands ready to give us an inheritance there, if it is but the country that we desire, and will choose, and diligently seek. God gives us our choice.[13] We may have our inheritance wherever we choose it, and may obtain heaven if we will but seek it by patient continuance in well-doing. We are all of us, as it were, placed here in this world as in a vast wilderness, with diverse countries about it, and with several ways or paths leading to these different countries, and we are left to our choice what course we will take. If we heartily choose heaven, and set our hearts entirely on that blessed Canaan—that land of love, and if we choose and love the path that leads to it, we may walk in that path; and if we continue to walk in it, it will lead us to heaven at last.

Let what we have heard of the land of love stir us all up to turn our faces toward it, and bend our course toward it. Is not what we have heard of the happy state of that country, and the many delights that are in it, enough to make us thirst after it, and to cause us, with the greatest earnestness and steadfastness of resolution, to press towards it, and spend our whole lives in travelling in the way that leads there? What joyful news might it well be to us when we hear of such a world of perfect peace and holy love, and to hear that it is possible, yea, that there is full opportunity, for us to come to it, and spend an eternity in its joys! Is not what we have heard of that blessed world enough to make us weary of this world of pride, and malice, and contention, and perpetual jarring and jangling, a world of confusion, a wilderness of hissing serpents, a tempestuous ocean, where there is no quiet rest, where all are for themselves, and selfishness reigns and governs, and all are striving to exalt themselves, regardless of what becomes of others, and all are eager after worldly good, which is the great object of desire and contention, and where men are continually annoying, and slandering, and reproaching, and otherwise injuring and abusing one another—a world full of injustice, and oppression, and cruelty—a world where there is so much treachery, and falsehood, and fickleness, and hypocrisy, and suffering, and death—where there is so little confidence in mankind, and every good man has so many failings, and has so much to render him unlovely and annoying, and where there is so much of sorrow, and guilt, and sin in every form.

Truly this is an evil world, and so it is destined to be. It is in vain for us to expect that it will be any other than a world of sin, a world of pride and enmity and strife, and so a restless world. And though the times may for a time be mended, yet these things will always be more or less found in the world so long as it stands. Who, then, would content himself with a portion in such a world? What man, acting wisely and considerately, would concern him-self much about laying up in store in such a world as this, and would not rather neglect this world, and let it go to them that would take it, and apply all his heart and strength to lay up treasure in heaven, and to press on to that world of love? What will it signify for us to hoard up great possessions in this world; and how can the thought of having our portion here be pleasing to us, when there is an allotment offered us in such a glorious world as heaven is, and especially when, if we have our portion here, we must, when the world has passed away, have our eternal portion in hell, that world of hatred, and of endless wrath of God, where only devils and damned spirits dwell?

We all naturally desire rest and quietness, and if we would obtain it, let us seek that world of peace and love of which we have now heard, where a sweet and blessed rest remains for God's true people. If we get an allotment in that world, then, when we have finished with this, we shall leave all our cares, and troubles, and fatigues, and perplexities, and disturbances forever. We shall rest from these storms that are raging here, and from every toil and labor, in the paradise of God. You that are poor, and think yourself despised by your neighbors and little cared for among men, do not much concern yourselves for this. Do not care much for the friendship of the world; but seek heaven, where there is no such thing as contempt, and where none are despised, but all are highly esteemed and honored, and dearly beloved by all. You who think you have met with many abuses, and much poor treat-ment from others, do not be concerned about it. Do not hate them for it, but set your heart on heaven, that world of love, and press toward that better country, where all is kindness and holy affection. And here *for direction how to seek heaven,*

First, Let not your heart go after the things of this world, as your chief good. Indulge not yourself in the possession of earthly things, as though they were able to satisfy your soul. This is the reverse of seeking heaven; it is to go in a way contrary to that which leads to the world of love. If you would seek heaven, your affections must be taken off from the pleasures of this world. You must not allow yourself in sensuality, or worldliness, or the pursuit of the enjoyments or honors of the world, or occupy your thoughts or time in heaping up the dust of the earth. You must mortify the desires of vain-glory, and become poor in spirit and lowly in heart.

Second, You must, in your meditations and holy exercises, be much engaged in conversing with heavenly persons, and objects, and enjoyments. You cannot constantly be seeking heaven, without having your thoughts much there. Turn, then, the stream of your thoughts and affections towards that world of love, and towards the God of love that dwells there, and toward the saints and angels that are at Christ's right hand. Let your thoughts, also, be much on the objects and enjoyments of the world of love. Commune much with God and Christ in prayer, and think often of all that is in heaven, of the friends who are there, and the praises and worship there, and of all that will make up the blessedness of that world of love. "Set your mind on things above, not on things on the earth" (Colossians 3:2).

Third, Be content to pass through all difficulties in the way to heaven. Though the path is before you, and you may walk in it if you desire, yet it is a way that is ascending, and filled with many difficulties and obstacles.[14] That glorious city of light and love is, as it were, on the top of a high hill or mountain, and there is no way to it but by upward and arduous steps. But though the ascent is difficult, and the way full of trials, still it is worth your while to meet them all for the sake of coming and dwelling in such a glorious city at last. Be willing, then, to undergo the labor, and meet the toil, and overcome the difficulty. What is it all in comparison with the sweet rest that is at your journey's end? Be willing to resist all the natural inclination of flesh and blood, which is downward, and press onward and upward to the prize. At every step it will be easier and easier to ascend; and the higher your ascent, the more will you be cheered by the glorious prospect before you, and by a nearer view of that heavenly city where, in a little while, you shall forever be at rest.

Fourth, In all your way let your eye be fixed on Jesus, who has gone to heaven as your forerunner. Look to Him. Behold His glory in heaven, that a sight of it may stir you up the more earnestly to desire to be there. Look to Him in His example. Consider how, by patient continuance in well-doing, and by patient endurance of great suffering, He went before you to heaven. Look to Him as your Mediator, and trust in the atonement which He has made, entering into the holiest of all in the upper temple. Look to Him as your intercessor, who forever pleads for you before the throne of God. Look to Him as your strength, that by His Spirit He may enable you to press on, and overcome every difficulty along the way. Trust in His promises of heaven to those that love and follow Him, which He has confirmed by entering into heaven as the head, and representative, and Savior of His people. And, finally,

Fifth, If you would be in the way to the world of love, see that you live a life of love—of love to God, and love to men. All of us hope to have part in the world of love hereafter, and therefore we should cherish the spirit of love, and live a life of holy love here on earth. This is the way to be like the inhabitants of heaven, who are now confirmed in love forever. Only in this way can you be like them in excellence and loveliness, and like them, too, in happiness, and rest, and joy. By living in love in this world you may be like them, too, in sweet and holy peace, and thus have, on earth, the fore-tastes of heavenly pleasures and delights. Thus, also, you may have a sense of the glory of heavenly things, as of God, and Christ, and holiness; and your heart be disposed and opened by holy love to God, and by the spirit of peace and love to men, to a sense of the excel-lence and sweetness of all that is to be found in heaven. Thus shall the windows of heaven be as it were opened, so that its glorious light shall shine in upon your soul. Thus you may have the evidence of your fitness for that blessed world, and that you are actually on the way to its possession. And being thus made fit, through grace, for the inheritance of the saints in light, when a few more days shall have passed away, you shall be with them in their blessedness forever. Happy, thrice happy those, who shall thus be found faithful to the end, and then shall be welcomed to the joy of their Lord! There "they shall hunger no more, neither thirst any more; neither shall the sun light on them, nor any heat. For the Lamb which is in the midst of the throne shall feed them, and lead them to living fountains of waters, and God shall wipe away all tears from their eyes" (Rev. 7:16,17). *AMEN!*

Endnotes

[1] See *Charity and its Fruits*, Lecture 15, pp. 304-322 (The Banner of Truth Trust, ISBN # 0 85151 009 4)

[2] The author is not intimating any moral imperfection or defect in the ministry or person of the Holy Spirit, but rather declaring that we have only received the earnest, or down-payment of the Spirit here (see Eph. 1:14). It is essential that we understand how strongly Edwards was convinced that the sign gifts were ended with the apostles! A careful study of *Charity and its Fruits* will clearly demonstrate that he was thoroughly convinced that the extraordinary gifts of the Spirit (tongues, miracles, prophecy etc.) were no longer operative in the church. He states, "Since the canon of Scripture has been completed, and the Christian Church fully founded and established, these extraordinary gifts have ceased" (p. 29).

[3] In his classic work *The Saints Everlasting Rest*, Richard Baxter spoke in similar exalted strains when contemplating the excellencies of our heavenly abode: "The fullness of joy is in God's immediate presence. We shall have light without a candle, and perpetual day without the sun; for "the city has no need of the sun, neither of the moon to shine in it; for the glory of God lightens it, and the Lamb is the light thereof; there shall be no night there, and they need no candle, neither light of the sun; and they shall reign forever and ever." To have needs, but no supply, is the condition of those in hell. To have needs supplied by means of creatures, is the condition of us on earth. To have needs supplied immediately from God, is the condition of the saints in heaven." Available through Soli Deo Gloria, Ligonier, PA.

[4] Edwards is not saying that all handicapped people will be excluded from entering heaven, but that those who were imperfect in any way, physically or emotionally or spiritually, will be without defect of any kind forever!

[5] John Bunyan, that immortal dreamer, thought much upon this theme, and once made the following observations concerning the perfectly lovely condition of our souls and bodies in glory: "I would discourse a little of the state of our body and soul in heaven, when we shall enjoy this blessed state of salvation. 1. Of the **soul**. It will be filled in all the faculties of it with as much bliss and glory as ever it can hold. The understanding will then be perfect in knowledge...Then shall our will and affections be ever in a burning flame of love to God and his Son Jesus Christ. Our love here hath ups and downs; but there it shall be always perfect with that perfection which is not possible in this world to be enjoyed. Then will our conscience have that peace and joy, that neither tongue or pen of men or angels can express. Then will our memory be so enlarged as to retain all things that happened to us in this world; so that with unspeakable aptness we shall call to mind all God's providences, all Satan's malice, all our weaknesses, all the rage of men, and how God made all work together for His glory and our good, to the everlasting ravishing of our hearts. 2. Of the **body**. It shall be raised in power, in incorruption, a spiritual body and glorious. It is compared to the brightness of the firmament, and to the shining of the stars forever and ever...And now when the body and soul are thus united, who can imagine what glory they both possess?" (*The Spiritual Riches of John Bunyan*, The World Publishing Co., 1952, *pp. 347,348*)

⁶ Although the first and great commandment is to love the Lord our God with *all* our heart and soul and strength (see Deut. 6:5; Matt. 22:37), there is no one who does this on this earth. Abraham Kuyper captures this truth in his wonderful devotional classic *To Be Near Unto God* (Baker): "Yea, it can freely be said, that your soul, as soon as it works normally, can not do otherwise than direct itself to God, in all its entirety and with all its strength. But nowhere does it show more strongly than in this very particular how abnormal in every way the soul has become by sin. And the worst of it is that with respect to this the soul itself is so little aware of its abnormality" (p. 172). In heaven, as Edwards points out here, the soul will finally be able to act "normally" in loving God with the "whole soul".

⁷ John Newton, author of *Amazing Grace*, wrote the following words on the theme of love to the brethren: "The principle of true love to the brethren is the LOVE OF GOD, that love which produces obedience, 1 Jn. 5:2. 'By this we know that we love the children of God, when we love God, and keep his commandments.' When people are free to form their connections and friendships, the ground of their communion is in a sameness of inclination. The love spoken of is spiritual. The children of God, who therefore stand in the relation of brethren to each other, though they have too many unhappy differences in points of smaller importance, agree in the supreme love they bear to their heavenly Father, and to Jesus their Savior; of course they agree in disliking and avoiding sin, which is contrary to the will and command of the God whom they love and worship. Upon these accounts they love one another, they are like-minded; and they live in a world where the bulk of mankind are against them, have no regard for their Beloved, and live in the sinful practices which His grace has taught them to hate. Their situation, therefore, increases their affection for each other. They are washed by the same blood, supplied by the same grace, opposed by the same enemies, and have the same heaven in view: therefore they love one another with a pure heart fervently." (*Letters of John Newton*, The Banner of Truth Trust). When one considers the fact that brother Newton spoke of the love of the brethren to each other on this earth, how much more glorious and perfect will its nature be in heaven, the world of love!

⁸ John Charles Ryle (1816-1900), in a sermon entitled *Heaven*, addressed this issue pointedly when he said: "You have heard of heaven; but all shall not enter it: and who are the persons who shall not enter in? Brethren, this is a sad and painful inquiry, and yet it is one that must be made. I can do no more than declare to you Scripture truth: it is not my fault if it is cutting and gives offence. I must deliver my Master's message and diminish nothing; the line I have to draw is not mine, but God's: the blame, if you will lay it, falls on the Bible not on me. "There shall in no wise enter into heaven any thing that defileth, neither whatsoever worketh abomination, or maketh a lie" (Revelation 21:27). Verily these are solemn words; they ought to make you think." (*The True Christian*, Baker, pp. 278,279)

⁹ In his monumental work *The City of God*, Augustine (354-430) concludes with a meditation upon the perfect peace and happiness of heaven in these words: "Who can measure the happiness of heaven, where no evil at all can touch us, no good will be out of reach; where life is to be one long laud extolling God, who will be all in all; where there will be no weariness to call for rest, no need to call for toil, no place for any energy but praise...In heaven, all glory will be true glory, since no one could ever err in praising

too little or too much. Perfect peace will reign, since nothing in ourselves or in any others will disturb this peace. . . God will be the source of every satisfaction, more than any heart can rightly crave, more than life and health, food and wealth, glory and honor, peace and every good—so that God, as St. Paul said, "may be all in all" (1 Cor. 15:28). He will be the consummation of all our desiring—the object of our unending vision, of our unlessening love, of our unwearying praise. And in this gift of vision, this response of love, this paean of praise, all alike will share, as all will share in everlasting life." (Book XXII, Chap. 30)

[10] For a detailed discussion of the entire subject of *Christian Assurance* see Thomas Brooks' fine work *Heaven on Earth* (The Banner of Truth Trust, ISBN # 0 85151 356 5).

[11] From this third mark set forth by Edwards one can readily see which side he would support in the present controversy over Lordship salvation. Edwards, along with the most reliable, and fruitful teachers since the Reformation, recognized what the writer of Hebrews meant when he declared: "Pursue peace with all men, and holiness, without which no one shall see the Lord" (12:14). How frightening that (so-called) evangelical teachers are seeking to defend a teaching which turns the grace of God into an excuse for lawlessness. This is the very issue Jude set out to address (see Jude 3f.).

[12] Edwards' sermon *Sinners in the Hands of an Angry God* power-fully confronts the unconverted with the fearful reality of standing on the brink of eternal destruction. For a free copy of this sermon please write to *Chapel Library, 2603 West Wright Street, Pensacola, FL 32505.*

[13] We must beware of mistaking the words of Edwards here to intimate the doctrine of Free Will which he clearly exposes as a lie and a cheat in his massive treatise: *Freedom of the Will* (see "*The Works of Jonathan Edwards: Vol. 1*", The Banner of Truth Trust, pp. 3-93).

[14] See the graphic picture of this set forth by John Bunyan in his classic work *The Pilgrim's Progress*, as he approaches, and must ascend Hill Difficulty if he is to make it to the Celestial City.

Recommended Works by Jonathan Edwards

The Works of Jonathan Edwards, two volumes, The Banner of Truth Trust, Carlisle, PA, ISBN # 0 85157 216 X

Charity and its Fruits, The Banner of Truth Trust, Carlisle, PA, ISBN # 0 85151 009 4, (not found in *The Works of Jonathan Edwards*)

The Experience that Counts!, abridged version of *Religious Affections*, Grace Publications, (Great Christian Classics # 11), London, England, ISBN # 0946462 23 2

The Rational Biblical Theology of Jonathan Edwards, by Dr. John Gerstner, three volumes, Berea Publications, Powhatan, VA, & Ligonier Ministries, Orlando, FL

Jonathan Edwards: A New Biography, by Iain Murray, The Banner of Truth Trust, Carlisle, PA, ISBN # 0 85151 494 4

The Mission of Calvary Press

The ministry of Calvary Press is firmly committed to printing quality Christian literature relevant to the dire needs of the church and the world at the dawn of the 21st century. We unashamedly stand upon the foundation stones of the Reformation of the 16th century—Scripture alone, Faith alone, Grace alone, Christ alone, and God's Glory alone!

Our prayer for this ministry is found in two portions taken from the Psalms: "And let the beauty of the LORD our God be upon us, And establish the work of our hands for us; Yes, establish the work of our hands," and "Not unto us, O LORD, not unto us, but to Your name give glory" (Ps. 90:17; 115:1).

For a complete catalog of all our titles,
please be sure to call us at
1-800-789-8175
or visit our new website:
calvarypress.com

HEAVEN
a world of love

John Piper, author of *Delighting God* writes: I believe with all my heart that in order to be useful in this world, we must fall in love with another world. In order to transform this world for the glory of Christ, we must be saturated with the glory and wisdom of another world. In order to be changed from one degree of glory to another now, we must hope fully in the grace that is about to be revealed to us soon. In order to be the light of the world, we must put our torch in the flame of heaven. In all of this, Jonathan Edwards is our great helper and *Heaven—A World of Love* is one of his greatest feasts." "Edwards gives us a taste of heaven that is savoring to the soul," writes **Dr. R.C. Sproul**, author, Chairman of Ligonier Ministries.

CALVARY PRESS PUBLISHING
PO BOX 805 · AMITYVILLE, NY 11701

Christian Life / Heaven
ISBN# 1-879737-36-1

Cover Design: Anthony Rotolo

9 781879 737365